Kandinsky **Cossacks**

ISBN O 946590 35 4
Published by order of the Trustees 1986
Copyright © 1986 The Tate Gallery All rights reserved
·Designed and published by Tate Gallery Publications,
Millbank, London SW1P 4RG
Printed by Balding + Mansell Limited, Wisbech, Cambs

PETER VERGO

Kandinsky **Cossacks**

THE TATE GALLERY

Foreword

'An American woman living in London has bought a pre-war painting from me and presented it to the Tate Gallery in London! It is the first truly modern painting in the famous museum in London. The painting is called "Cosaques" . . .' Thus Wassily Kandinsky, in a letter to Galka Scheyer of 13 January 1939. The generous American was Mrs Hazel McKinley, sister of Peggy Guggenheim. 'Cossacks' was not only one of the first modern paintings to be acquired by a museum anywhere in Britain, it was also the first example of German Expressionist art to enter a public collection in this country. The paintings of Franz Marc and Lyonel Feininger at Leicester Art Gallery were bought slightly later, in 1944, from an exhibition organised by the museum's far-sighted director, Trevor Thomas.

'Cossacks' was shown in the large exhibition of *20th century German Art* at the New Burlington Galleries in London in July 1938. This exhibition signalled a brave attempt by a group of sympathisers led by the critic Herbert Read openly to affirm their support for those modern artists who were being persecuted, forced into exile or forbidden to exhibit by Hitler. At Munich the previous summer the Nazis' notorious exhibition of 'Degenerate' Art (*Entartete Kunst*), consisting of 730 works out of a total of nearly 16,000 confiscated from German museums, had been visited by some two million people. In 1938 it was still travelling round Germany and in July of that year could be seen at Berlin.

The London exhibition, by contrast, was made up of works borrowed from private collections outside Germany. It is interesting to note that the organisers at one point considered showing works by artists who had compromised with the National Socialist regime, but later dropped the idea. At the opening, in the words of one who was present, 'Elizabeth Schumann sang Schubert and Wolf . . . and there was such enthusiasm and such emotion because of what was happening in Germany that she went on and on till nearly midnight'. Kandinsky, by that time living in Paris, was represented by six oils (from 1909 to 1930) and four watercolours, in addition to 'Cossacks'. Major works by Beckmann[1], Corinth, Kirchner, Klee, Kokoschka[2], Lehmbruck, Liebermann, Marc, Modersohn Becker, Pechstein and others were displayed alongside paintings and sculpture by fifteen artists who had already emigrated to Britain, including Martin Bloch, Georg Ehrlich and Hein Heckroth. Kandinsky's 'Cossacks' appears to have been the only important work in the exhibition to end up in a British public gallery.

[4]

Wassily Kandinsky (1866–1944)
Cossacks 1910–11
Oil on canvas, 94.5 × 130cm
Presented to the Tate Gallery by
Mrs Hazel McKinley 1938

Peter Vergo was one of the organisers of the exhibition *Abstraction: Towards a New Art* held at the Tate Gallery in 1980. He has more recently co-edited and translated into English Kandinsky's writings on art. We are grateful to him for his illuminating interpretation of a painting which, for the reasons outlined above, occupies a unique place in the history of modern art collecting in this country. We would also like to thank Faber and Faber Limited for permission to reprint as an appendix Dr Vergo's translation of Kandinsky's essay on 'Composition 4'.

Richard Calvocoressi
Assistant Keeper, Modern Collection

[1] including his triptych 'Temptation' 1937 (now Staatsgalerie moderner Kunst, Munich).
[2] for example, the portrait of 'Herwath Walden' 1910 (now Staatsgalerie, Stuttgart) and the 'Self portrait of a Degenerate Artist' 1937.

For Kenneth Lindsay

Kandinsky Cossacks

'Sketch' and Picture

Immediately striking by virtue of its size and the luminosity of its colours, precious because it remains the only early Kandinsky in a British public collection, the Tate Gallery's 'Cossacks' poses a succession of riddles. Neither its title nor its date can be established with complete certainty. It is signed and dated, not once but twice (on front and back) 'Kandinsky 1910'; but the artist's 'house catalogues', the lists he kept as a record of his own paintings, show that the picture was done on 13 January 1911. The name 'Cossack' or 'Cossacks' derives from traditional usage, and from an old label stuck on the back of the picture; but in Kandinsky's house-catalogues, the work is entitled 'Schlacht' (Battle). Also on the back of the canvas is written in the artist's hand: 'Zu Komposition 4 (Fragment)'.[1]

How best to interpret this inscription turns out to be a matter of some consequence. 'Cossacks' has often been termed a 'sketch' for 'Composition 4', Kandinsky's most important painting of early 1911, to which he likewise gave the subsidiary title 'Battle'.[2] And indeed, the house-catalogues reveal that 'Cossacks' was finished several weeks prior to the completion of 'Composition 4', while the phrase 'zu Komposition 4' also suggests something done in advance of or preparatory to the final picture.

The series of paintings to which the artist gave the name 'composition' – seven in all during the years before 1914 – occupied a very special place within his work and thought. In his autobiographical essay 'Reminiscences', he recorded that the word itself affected him with a sense of reverence, like a prayer.[3] And in his major theoretical statement of this pre-war period, *On the Spiritual in Art*, he described his 'compositions' as a kind of painting in which 'reason, the conscious, the deliberate, and the purposeful play a preponderant role', and as having been 'slowly and almost deliberately worked out' by means of preliminary sketches.[4]

But despite the evident relationship between 'Cossacks' and 'Composition 4', to call the Tate picture a 'sketch' is misleading in several important respects. There is nothing 'sketchy' about it. It reveals no hesitations, no uncertainties, no changes of mind. The underlying conception was clearly fully formed in the artist's mind before ever he put brush to canvas. Even at first sight, the picture is remarkable for its

1 **Improvisation Deluge** 1913
Städtische Galerie im Lenbachhaus, Munich

2 **Study for Composition 7** 1913
Felix Klee, Berne

3 **Study for Composition 7 (No.3)** 1913
Städtische Galerie im Lenbachhaus, Munich

high degree of finish and the clarity and logic of its structure. Nor can it really be called a 'variant' of 'Composition 4'. It does not propose an alternative solution to the compositional problems Kandinsky faced in grappling with the latter work. Rather, it reproduces, almost exactly, the upper left-hand portion of 'Composition 4', on a very similar scale, the principal differences between the two 'versions' being in the compositional details of the upper corners of 'Cossacks', and in the zig-zag motif which dominates the topmost part of that picture, usually identified as a highly-stylized flight of birds.

Kandinsky was not, in any case, a great one for changing his mind. Few of his paintings, even those usually termed 'sketches' or 'studies', betray any sign of corrections or afterthoughts. This in itself need not surprise us unduly. Other artists on occasion have made elaborate, often highly finished oil studies for major pictures, Constable being the obvious example. On the other hand, while the large-format oil sketches for Kandinsky's immediately ensuing 'Compositions' – 'No.5' (1911), 'No.6' (1913), 'No.7' (1913) – all share the same highly finished character as 'Cossacks', none shows merely a partial view.[5] On the contrary, all reveal, with a greater or lesser degree of fidelity, the intended compositional structure of the final painting.

Equally striking is the fact that many of Kandinsky's drawings exhibit the same elaborate, highly finished character as the so-called 'studies' for the great 'Compositions'. Presentation drawings apart, for many, even most artists drawing is an exploratory medium, an opportunity to test first ideas, to correct and discard. But Kandinsky's drawings rarely have anything in the least exploratory or tentative about them. With few exceptions, they exude an air of confidence, of something fully worked-out in advance, betraying little of the artist's intentions, or of the way a given painting evolved.[6] This is especially true of the drawings and studies for 'Composition 4', of which some half-dozen survive, not counting a couple of related works which clearly do not precede, but derive from the final picture: a line etching published in the *Blue Rider Almanac* of 1912 (hand-coloured in the de-luxe edition),[7] and a black-and-white woodcut design for the cover of a Russian portfolio.[8] Even what appears to be the earliest of the drawings (fig.4), showing merely the skeleton of the composition, betrays neither hesitations nor corrections, but appears to reflect a conception already fully fashioned in the artist's mind: an *aide-memoire* rather than a voyage of discovery. Nor do there seem to be any drawings at all related to the Tate's 'Cossacks'.

For the present, we should simply note the curious, highly finished character of the drawings and studies, since it is important for an understanding of Kandinsky's method of working at this time.

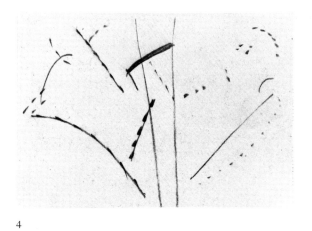

4

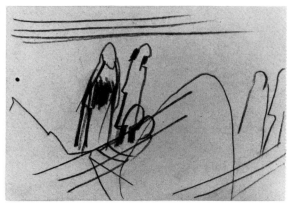

5

6

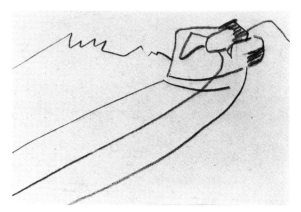

7

8

4–9 **Six drawings for Composition 4**
*Musée national d'art moderne, Paris,
Nina Kandinsky Bequest, 1981*

9

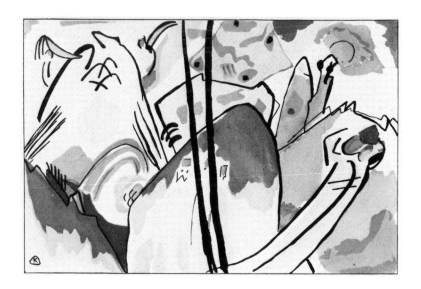

Kandinsky on Kandinsky

Usually, Kandinsky was far readier to talk about the tasks of art in general than about his own art in particular. By nature, he was extremely reserved, even secretive. He admitted on more than one occasion that he hated to have to underline the meaning of his pictures, and that he did not want his works to be like raucous street-vendors who plaster their barrows with all kinds of gaudy advertisement.[9] But in autumn 1913, Herwarth Walden, owner of the Sturm gallery in Berlin, published the first book devoted wholly to Kandinsky: an album comprising reproductions of 67 of the artist's works, together with the German version of his autobiographical 'Reminiscences'.[10] This 'Sturm album' also contained, by way of an appendix, three shorter essays by Kandinsky about individual paintings: 'Composition 4', 'Composition 6' and the so-called 'Picture with White Edge'.[11]

Of the three essays, that concerning 'Composition 4', written in 1911, is the earliest. It is also very different from its companion pieces, which were not written until 1913. By comparison with their flowing narrative, it is couched in a jerky, staccato style, a bit like an extended telegram. The later essays, moreover, tell us a good deal about the genesis of the two pictures: how 'Composition 6' evolved from a now-lost glass-painting of the Deluge, and how the artist wrestled for months with the compositional problems posed by 'Picture with White Edge'. But in his piece on 'Composition 4', Kandinsky limits himself purely to formal and iconographic analysis, giving no indication how ideas for the picture crystallised in his mind, nor of the stages by which the work was brought to completion. He also says nothing about any studies or sketches, nor about 'Cossacks'. Ironically, the only clue to his intentions in painting the latter picture is to be gleaned, not from his essay on 'Composition 4', but from a passing remark about 'Composition 6'. Here, Kandinsky observed, the painting comprised two centres which had 'grown together', but which remained compositionally so distinct that the work might still be divided into two independent pictures. Could it be that, at some point in the evolution of 'Composition 4', he wished to determine whether the left-hand part of that painting might likewise be treated independently, whether it was, so to speak, compositionally fitted for survival?

But if Kandinsky offers no clue to his intentions, nor to the evolution of the picture, his analysis of 'Composition 4' is revealing in other ways. He discusses, for example, the manner in which colour fails to correspond to contour, flowing over and beyond the outlines of form. He describes the 'tensions' which operate in different parts of the composition, and the contrast between 'angular movement' and 'light-cold-sweet colours'. He also points to a number of quite specific motifs which play an important role in the picture: the entangled lines in the upper left-hand corner which represent battling horsemen, the castle on a hill which dominates the centre of the composition, at lower right a pair of reclining figures, and the two vertical black lines dividing the two halves of the painting, which Kandinsky identifies as 'spears' or 'lances'. For our part, we may begin to isolate other motifs of which the artist himself makes no mention: the large standing figures on a hill to the right of the castle, and the shadowy forms which occupy the lower centre of the composition, who gradually resolve themselves as three people, two of then grasping the vertical black lances. Their red hats and yellow hands also help us to identify with greater certainty the 'battling forms' at the

11 **Composition 4** 1911, *Kunstsammlung Nordrhein-Westfalen, Düsseldorf*

upper left, since the two rider figures likewise have red hats and yellow hands which in this case are holding long curved purple sabres. Also in this 'warlike' zone of the painting we may, perhaps more tentatively, identify the 'spiky' forms at the extreme left of the composition as guns, or possibly parts of a palisade.[12]

Kandinsky and Abstraction

Kandinsky's original purpose in formulating his essay on 'Composition 4' remains unclear. He would sometimes jot down brief notes on individual paintings – more, one suspects, for himself than for the public: his essay on the picture he called 'Impression 2 (Moscow)', for example, which remains unpublished to this day.[13] On the other hand, in allowing his description of 'Composition 4' to appear in the 'Sturm album' of 1913, he might well have hoped to do something to counter the rising tide of incomprehension which had greeted his recent work. He had been derided in the German press as a charlatan and a fraud.[14] To jeer at his painting had become something of a fashion – and not just in Germany. One reviewer, writing in the *Scotsman*, described certain of his 'Improvisations', shown at the Salon des Indépendants in 1912, as 'looking as if a dog dipped its feet or its tail, or both, in the palette, and walked across the canvas.'[15]

Much of this antagonism resulted from the illogical but widespread assumption that Kandinsky's work was abstract, and therefore meaningless. Even a painting like 'Composition 2', in which human figures and animals abound, had been dismissed by one Munich critic as passable only if intended as a 'colour sketch for a modern carpet'.[16] 'Composition 4', a picture likewise based on representational forms which are, however, much harder to identify at first sight, was apparently quite incomprehensible. Years later, the artist himself recalled in a letter to Hans Hildebrandt that he found it extraordinary, and at the same time indicative of visual attitudes in those days, that the public was simply unable to discern the objective basis of a work like 'Composition 4'.[17] Thus, one aim in publishing his essay was doubtless to open the viewer's eyes to the presence of identifiable subject matter in the painting. On the other hand, Kandinsky was adamant that objects in pictures should not be too clear. His main criticism of traditional narrative painting was that recognition of an all-too-familiar story, or of hackneyed imagery, could easily blind the spectator to the purely 'abstract' language of colour and form – a language whose nuances interested him more and more as he came to distance himself increasingly from representational aims.

Perhaps the clearest account of his position at this time is to be found in the manuscript notes Kandinsky prepared for an autobiographical lecture he was supposed to deliver in Cologne in January 1914. In these notes, the artist makes clear that for him, the mastery of abstract form had been the outcome of years of bitter struggle, that for a long time he had, in his own words, been 'unable to experience purely abstract form without bridging the gap by means of objects'. Objects, Kandinsky wrote, remained important to him because of their 'particular spiritual sound which can – and does – serve as material for all realms of art.' On the other hand, he was anxious that the objects in his paintings should 'not all be recognized at once, in order that their spiritual overtones might be experienced gradually by the spectator, one after the other.' For this reason, by his own account he 'dissolved' objects to a greater or lesser extent within the same picture, just as we see in 'Composition 4', causing colours to flow over and beyond the boundaries of form, and abbreviating forms themselves to the very limits of legibility.[18]

In this 'veiling and stripping' of imagery, as it has been termed,[19] in his works from 1911 onwards, Kandinsky went further than he perhaps realised. He seems to have been largely unaware just how difficult his contemporaries, even those well-disposed towards his art, found it to understand these pictures. And not just his contemporaries. During the 1920s and '30s, many of Kandinsky's paintings of these years before the First World War continued to be regarded as unequivocally abstract, perhaps because the artist himself had by then become convinced that he created his first non-representational work as early as 1910 or 1911.[20] Those few intelligent observers who still claimed to see vestiges of representational form in these paintings were, for the most part, dismissed by art historians and critics who now hailed Kandinsky as the 'inventor' of abstract painting.

12 **Composition 6** 1913
State Hermitage Museum, Leningrad

Motif and Method

13 Vasily Koren, Plate from an Apocalypse Woodcut from D. Rovinsky, *Russkie Narodnie Kartinki*, St Petersburg, 1881

In fact, few if any of Kandinsky's works of the period before 1914 are entirely abstract. Sometimes, the motifs on which they are based are so disguised as to be well-nigh illegible; but it is nearly always possible to trace such motifs back to some earlier and more legible rendering. For example, three oarsmen in a coracle-like boat occur with surprising frequency in Kandinsky's paintings of 1912 and 1913. In its most cryptic form, this motif is to be found in the great apocalyptic 'Compositions', Nos. '6' and '7', of 1913 where, reduced to a mere hieroglyph, it could scarcely be recognised without prior knowledge. Its occurence in this particular context suggests that the motif of the rowers may have had its ultimate source in a plate from a woodcut apocalypse by the Russian seventeenth-century master Vasily Koren, published in an anthology of folk woodcuts, or *lubki*, almost certainly known to Kandinsky.[21] But in less impenetrable guise, the same motif recurs in a variety of other works: in the bottom right hand corner of the glass-painting 'With Sun', and in the closely related oils, 'Improvisation 21a' (1911) and 'Small Pleasures'; but also in its own right, as the subject of the picture, in 'Improvisation 26' of 1912.[22]

The rowers is one of a small number of motifs which enjoy an especially wide currency in Kandinsky's work at this time, and which evidently had a particular emotional significance for the artist. It is also noticeable that his tendency to employ emotionally highly charged motifs became more and more marked, the more closely he approached

14 **With Sun** 1910, oil on glass
Städtische Galerie im Lenbachhaus, Munich

towards abstraction: motifs, for the most part, related to subjects such as the deluge, the last judgment and the resurrection. The relatively limited number of motifs he uses have, however, virtually unlimited potential for re-utilization, recurring again and again in different contexts and combinations, in works in a wide variety of media – more abbreviated, perhaps, but without any very significant change in appearance. Hence the curiously 'non-preparatory' character of the studies, so called, of this period, whether drawings, watercolours or oils. Their highly finished, fully worked-out appearance is due precisely to the fact that the motifs on which they are based were already long since established, not needing further elaboration by means of studies in the conventional sense. Instead, almost every drawing or glass-painting or oil 'study' was, in effect, a further elaboration of the works immediately preceding it and, at the same time, a preparation for those which were to follow.

Kandinsky's method of working, by way of chains or sequences of motivically related compositions, means that it is necessary to look across a wide range of works, rather than at works in isolation, in order to understand the significance of the motifs they contain. For example, the ubiquitous horsemen, by far the most frequently used motif at this period, are not always battling horsemen as in 'Cossacks', but sometimes apocalyptic horsemen, or jockeys, or St George and the Dragon

15 **Improvisation 21a** 1911
Städtische Galerie im Lenbachhaus, Munich

16 Vignette from *On the Spiritual in Art*
woodcut

as in 'Picture with White Edge'.[23] The 'reclining figures' in the bottom right-hand corner of 'Composition 4' are a case in point. Kandinsky himself does no more than allude to their presence, and says nothing that might elucidate their meaning. But similar forms, though by no means as widespread as the motif of the rowers, occur elsewhere in Kandinsky's *oeuvre*. The woodcut that decorates the beginning of the third chapter of his treatise, *On the Spiritual in Art*, is based on an almost identical motif which resolves itself as a pair of embracing figures (clearer still in the preparatory drawing for this vignette). The theme of embrace plays an important role in the artist's work at this time. One of the dominant motifs of his glass-painting 'All Saints' Day' is a pair of embracing saints, whose recognizable shape persists in more 'abstract' treatments of the same subjects (compare the oil painting of the same title, fig. 21), and who are also lifted from their original context to form, by themselves, one of the colour woodcuts from Kandinsky's poetry and prints album *Klänge*. The extended forms of the reclining figures in 'Composition 4' also recur, more compressed but performing a very similar compositional function, in the painting 'Improvisation 27' (subtitled 'Garden of Love'), and in a watercolour now in the Guggenheim Museum, identified as a study for another oil, 'Improvisation 25', which likewise bears the subtitle 'Garden of Love'.[24] Since the 'spiritual overtones' of a given motif inevitably carry across from one painting to the next, the spirit of amity, of reconciliation and of love embodied in these latter paintings presumably attaches also to the reclining figures as they appear, albeit in a quite different pictorial context, at lower right in 'Composition 4'.

Occultism and Revolution

Kandinsky, as already mentioned, says nothing in his essay on 'Composition 4' about the meaning of the picture, nor about 'Cossacks'. The only contemporary reference which gives some clue as to what may have been in his mind occurs in a letter from his mistress, Gabriele Münter, dated 20 August 1912. Writing to the composer Arnold Schoenberg in Berlin, Münter reports that she has been reading a book entitled *Siderische Geburt* by the German mystical writer Volker.[25] Though admitting that she is finding it rather slow going ('like a heavy gold chain passing through my hands link by link'), she recommends the book to Schoenberg ('I believe there is something there for you') and, in a postscript, specifically likens the content of Volker's treatise to that of Kandinsky's paintings, particularly 'Compositions 2', '4' and '5'.[26]

Given Kandinsky's well-known interest in mysticism, it is hardly surprising to find that he too had read *Siderische Geburt* at about this time. He even recommended it to his painter friend Franz Marc, as

17 **Small Pleasures** 1913
Solomon R. Guggenheim Museum, New York

18 **Improvisation 26** 1912
Städtische Galerie im Lenbachhaus, Munich

emerges from a letter of 1 September 1911 from Marc to his wife Maria.[27] A copy of the book was found among the contents of Kandinsky's Munich library, along with a good deal of other occult and theosophical literature.[28] Much that it contains, especially its constant reiteration of the themes of spiritual regeneration and the rejection of the corporeal, would have found an immediate echo in Kandinsky's contemporary preoccupation with the turn away from materialism and the dawn of a new spiritual era.

Kandinsky himself, however, makes no allusion to Volker in connection with 'Composition 4', and his only other reference to the picture occurs much later, in his letter of March 1927 to Hans Hildebrandt mentioned above.[29] Here, in addition to castigating the 'visual attitudes' of the pre-war public, he lets slip, almost in passing, an intriguing aside: that 'Composition 4' had its origin in a charge of cossacks through the streets of Moscow he had witnessed during the ill-fated Russian revolution in 1905.

This passing remark is clearly important for any interpretation of the picture. Yet, like so much else Kandinsky says, it seems to pose almost as many problems as it solves. Whatever else it may be, 'Composition 4' is certainly not a literal rendering of the scene the artist describes, a charge of cossacks through a city street. There is no city, only a castle on a hill, and the only mounted figures are the two horsemen engaged in single combat in the upper left-hand corner of the painting. Other elements in the painting bear no evident relationship to any 'revolutionary' theme: the reclining couple at lower right, for example, or the huge figures on the hillside above them, perhaps related to the 'yellow giants' Kandinsky specifies in the stage directions for his play *Yellow Sound*.[30]

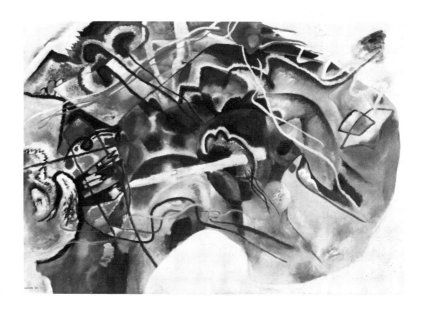

19 **Picture with White Edge** 1913
Solomon R. Guggenheim Museum, New York

The only other figures that might be identified as cossacks, because their garb is similar to that of the battling horsemen, are those occupying the foreground of the picture, and they are neither riding nor charging, but merely standing, or possibly pacing up and down, rather like a ceremonial guard of honour.

Secondly, a purely historical problem attaches to Kandinsky's recollection. The artist was not, as far as is known, in Moscow at all during 1905, and there are no paintings, drawings or documents which might convincingly be associated with any visit. He did, however, travel to Odessa together with his father in early October of that year; exactly how long he stayed is not clear, except that he was back in Germany by mid-November.[31] The strikes and demonstrations of that Russian autumn would then have been at their height, and it is perfectly possible that Kandinsky indeed witnessed some scene such as that he described to Hildebrandt more than twenty years later, either in Odessa or during a brief, otherwise unrecorded trip to Moscow. Equally, it is possible he had read or heard about a similar confrontation between cossacks and strikers, and his vivid visual imagination succeeded subsequently in convincing him that he had actually been witness to such an event.

Kandinsky is not usually thought to have been an overtly political artist. There are, however, in his writings a number of references and allusions which suggest at least a measure of political involvement. His autobiographical 'Reminiscences', though rarely specific, make clear his interest in political events during his student days at Moscow

20 **All Saints' Day** 1911, oil on glass
Städtische Galerie im Lenbachhaus, Munich

University. Kandinsky recalls with approval the students' struggle against the 'cunning and undisguised universities bill of 1855', and the subsequent creation of a pan-student organisation. He also confesses that these 'purely human disturbances' left him not an hour's peace, keeping his soul in a 'state of constant vibration'.[32] And when, in 1917, the Bolshevik revolution came in earnest, he for a time allied himself with the cause, being closely associated with Lunacharsky's Commissariat of Enlightenment, and no doubt seeing the establishment of the Institute of Artistic Culture in Moscow, initially under his own directorship, as an opportunity of reforming art education and artistic policy generally in newly post-revolutionary Russia.[33]

Kandinsky's last four pre-war 'Compositions' (Nos. 4, 5, 6 and 7) have been seen by a number of commentators as linked in content and imagery, sharing, in very general terms, a common apocalyptic or eschatological theme.[34] More accurate might be to describe them all as 'revolutionary' in content, not in the narrow sense of purely political revolution, but in the more extended sense that all four paintings are concerned, one way or another, with dramatic, even violent change, with the attainment through conflict and contradiction of a new spiritual awareness, symbolised by the 'battle' which provides one of the alternative titles for 'Composition 4'. It is in this context that the artist's recollection regarding the historical origin of 'Composition 4' becomes relevant: like many Russian liberals, Kandinsky surely saw the abortive revolution of 1905 as harbinger of change, of a new social order, perhaps even the first sign of that 'spiritual turning-point' he described in his book *On the Spiritual in Art*.

Kandinsky, Wagner and Schopenhauer

But whereas we may search Kandinsky's paintings in vain for any reference to revolutionary hordes or charging cossacks, both 'Composition 4' and the Tate's 'Cossacks' contain one allusion so specific that it is surprising it has provoked so little comment. What, after all, are we to make of the central motif of a castle on a hill, separated from us by a chasm spanned by a rainbow bridge? Is this not Valhalla, the castle of the Gods, paid for by violence and deceit, exactly as Wagner shows it to us in the closing scene of *Das Rheingold*, the first part of his tetralogy *The Ring of the Nibelung*? This final scene, starting with Donner's mighty hammerblow which dispels the mists above the river Rhine, and ending with the procession of the Gods across the rainbow bridge to take possession of the castle, must surely have made a vivid impression on someone of Kandinsky's visual sensitivity, as indeed it has done over the decades on so many artists fortunate enough to have witnessed all but the most 'abstract' productions of Wagner's masterpiece.

Towards the end of his life, Kandinsky's early enthusiasm for Wagner had evidently waned to a large extent. Nina Kandinsky recalled that their collection of gramophone records contained no recordings of Wagner, and that Kandinsky could only be persuaded, under duress, on one occasion during their entire stay in Paris to attend a performance of one of the composer's operas, because their friend Franz von Hoesslin was conducting and had expressly invited them.[35] But there can be little doubt that, during the Blue Rider years, Kandinsky was much engrossed by Wagner. His essay 'On Stage Composition', published in the *Blue Rider Almanac*, demonstrates his familiarity both with the composer's theories and with his musical practice.[36] It includes a number of detailed remarks on the use of the *Leitmotif* in Wagner's operas, as well as on what Kandinsky regarded as the disadvantages of the composer's 'additive' method of reinforcing one form of artistic experience with another (though there is an evident similarity between Wagner's conception of the *Gesamtkunstwerk* and what Kandinsky termed the 'monumental art of the future', a coming-together of all the arts which would occur, ideally, on the stage). And in 'Reminiscences', the artist recalled one of his formative experiences as a student, witnessing a performance of *Lohengrin* at the Bolshoi Theatre in Moscow:

> *Lohengrin* seemed to me the complete realisation of that [fairy-tale] Moscow. The violins, the deep tones of the basses, and especially the wind-instruments at that time embodied for me all the power of that pre-nocturnal hour. I saw all my colours in my mind, they stood before my eyes. Wild, almost crazy lines were sketched in front of me . . . It became . . . quite clear to me that art in general was far more powerful than I had thought . . . that painting could develop just such powers as music possesses.[37]

Interestingly, in the 1918 Russian version of 'Reminiscences', Kandinsky added a footnote to this passage, referring to what he now terms the 'sickly sentimentality' and 'superficiality of this, the weakest of Wagner's operas.' On the other hand, he also remarks in passing that *Tristan* and *The Ring* held his critical faculties 'in thrall for many a long year by their power and uniqueness of expression.'[38] This note not only reflects, at least as far as *Lohengrin* is concerned, a fairly radical change of mind. It also, like so many of Kandinsky's asides, adds significantly to our knowledge and understanding. It suggests, in particular, why he might have found Wagner appealing, that is to say not just for musical but also for philosophical reasons. For Wagner's mature operas, *Tristan* and *The Ring* in particular, are like Kandinsky's theoretical writings pervaded by echoes of a quite specific philosophical tradition – a world view which, as Wagner himself readily admitted, drew in almost all important respects on the writings of Schopenhauer, especially the philosopher's major treatise, *The World as Will and Idea.*

It has become something of a commonplace to refer to the Schopenhauerian content of *Tristan and Isolde*, not least since the composer himself left so detailed an account of his intentions, couched in un-mistakably Schopenhauerian language: 'I immersed myself only in the depths of the inner motions of the soul and . . . created from out of this most secret kernel of the world its outward form . . . life and death, the whole existence of the external world are here dependent on inner movements.'[39] But *The Ring*, too, is pervaded by Schopenhauer, as its composer was quick to realise. In fact, Wagner first encountered *The World as Will and Idea* only after he had begun work on *Das Rheingold*, the first of the four operas, but it soon dawned on him that much of what he found in Schopenhauer's treatise he had already incorporated, albeit unconsciously, in his conception of *The Ring*.[40] And indeed, *Rheingold* itself contains a number of exact parallels, conscious or unconscious, with elements of Schopenhauerian philosophy. To take a single example: consider the equivocal light in which Wagner portrays science, personified in the devious character of Loge. It is Loge who makes possible the theft of Alberich's magic ring, but in so doing, he wishes on the world a terrible weapon whose power he himself cannot control. He is also given to promising what he cannot fulfil, as in his undertaking to restore to the Rhinemaidens the stolen gold – an undertaking Wotan dismisses with the contemptuous retort: 'Your promises don't commit me!' But Wotan too is doomed, and with him the eternal Gods, for having once possessed the fatal Ring – helpless victims of Alberich's indomitable curse.

23 **Study for Improvisation 25** water-colour, *Solomon R. Guggenheim Museum, New York*

24 **Improvisation 27** 1912
Metropolitan Museum, New York

Kandinsky's ambivalence towards the methods of rational and scientific enquiry, in particular his belief that positivistic science had led mankind into an impasse, in part reflects his contemporary pre-occupation with theosophy and mysticism. His disillusionment finds expression in one of the most evocative passages in 'Reminiscences', in which he describes his feeling that science had been 'destroyed . . . an error of the learned, who were not building their divine edifice stone by stone with steady hands, by transfigured light, but were groping at random for truth in the darkness and blindly mistaking one object for another.'[41] But there are other passages, too, in his more specifically theoretical writings in which his debt to the philosophy of German Idealism, and especially to Schopenhauerian thought, is unmistakable. In *The World as Will and Idea*, Schopenhauer had drawn a fundamental distinction, not only between scientific and aesthetic knowledge, but also between our normal, everyday manner of looking at the world and what he termed a state of 'pure, willess contemplation'. The same distinction underlies much of Kandinsky's treatise, *On the Spiritual in Art*, as for instance in the passage in which he describes what he terms the principles of the 'new ballet':

> A very simple movement, whose purpose is unknown, produces of its own accord a significant, mysterious and solemn effect . . . provided that one is unaware of the external, practical purpose of the movement. Then it has the effect of a pure sound. A simple, concerted action . . . produces, if its purpose is unknown, an effect so significant, so mysterious and dramatic and striking, that one involuntarily stops still as if in the presence of a vision, of life upon another plane – until all of a sudden the magic vanishes, the practical explanation comes like a bolt from the blue, and the mysterious procedure and the reasons behind it are laid bare. In this simple movement, which to all external appearances is unmotivated, lies an immeasurable wealth of possibilities.[42]

And in general, the belief that art is capable of revealing truths inaccessible to science, above all, that it is the task of art to give an account of *inner* experience, is central not merely to Kandinsky's theory of art, but to the aesthetics of the German Expressionist movement as a whole.

Conclusion

To find Wagnerian references embedded alongside philosophical and mystical allusions in a picture supposedly inspired by the 1905 Russian revolution need not surprise us unduly. In his essay on 'Composition 6', which is in so many ways revealing of his working methods at this time, Kandinsky admits to his fondness for 'mingling' disparate kinds of imagery. The same tactic is used in many of his other pre-1914 paintings: the juxtaposition of the well-worn motif of the troika with that of St George and the dragon, for example, in 'Picture with White Edge', or the apocalyptic rider who makes a dramatic incursion into the summer-holiday outing depicted in the painting known as 'Improvisation "Gorge"' of 1914.[43] Kandinsky not only expected his paintings to produce their effect gradually, after prolonged contemplation, as the imagery on which they are based slowly insinuated itself into the viewer's consciousness. He also clearly intended them to work on a number of different levels, so that to see the various layers of meaning contained within a picture such as 'Composition 4' as somehow incompatible would be to miss the point – the point being that Kandinsky's major paintings are not susceptible of any single, definitive interpretation; rather, they lend themselves to numerous interpretations.

But in fact, the multifarious sources on which the artist draws in the making of 'Composition 4' are remarkably consistent as regards what Kandinsky would have considered their inner significance. Volker's treatise *Siderische Geburt* (subtitled 'A Seraphic Quest from the Death of the World to the Baptism of the Deed'), which Münter regarded as so similar in content to Kandinsky's 'Compositions', is concerned with spiritual regeneration and the destruction of the established order of materialism. As we have seen, Kandinsky's hopes of a rebirth or 'turning-point' kindled by the stirrings of revolution would have been first and foremost spiritual, not political in character. And, after all, what is Wagner's *Ring of the Nibelung* about, if not the passing of the old order? And, of course, about the power of love. Nothing in Kandinsky's work is the product of coincidence, least of all the fact that the 'reclining figures' absent in the Tate's 'Cossacks', but which occur at lower right in 'Composition 4', derive from the artist's earlier treatments of the traditional theme of the Garden of Love or Garden of Delights, enabling us with reasonable certainty to substitute for the artist's unrevealing label our own more telling identification 'loving couple'.[44]

Appendix

Supplementary definition

1. Masses (Weights)

   > lower centre – blue (gives the whole picture a cold tone)
   > upper right – divided blue, red, yellow
   > upper left – black lines of the entangled horses
   > lower right – extended lines of the reclining figures

2. Contrasts

   > between mass and line
   > between precise and blurred
   > between entangled line and entangled colour and
   > p r i n c i p a l contrast: between angular, sharp movement (battle)
   >   and light-cold-sweet colours

3. Running-over

   > of colour beyond the outlines
   > Only the complete contour of the c a s t l e is diminished by the
   > way in which the sky flows in over its outline

4. Two centres

   > 1. Entangled lines
   > 2. Acute form modelled in blue
   >
   > separated from one another by the two vertical black lines (lances).

The whole composition is intended to produce a very bright effect, with many sweet colours, which often run into one another (resolution), while the yellow, too, is cold. The juxtaposition of this bright-sweet-cold tone with angular movement (battle) is the principal contrast in the picture. It seems to me that this contrast is here, by comparison with *Composition 2*, more powerful, but at the same time harder (inwardly), clearer, the a d v a n t a g e of which is that it produces a more precise effect, the d i s a d v a n t a g e being that this precision has too great a clarity.

*   *   *

The following are the basic elements of the composition:

1. C o n c o r d of passive masses.
2. P a s s i v e movement principally to the right and upward.

3. Mainly a c u t e movement to the left and upward.

4. C o u n t e r - m o v e m e n t s in both directions (the movement to the right is contradicted by smaller forms that move toward the left, and so on).

5. C o n c o r d between masses and lines that simply recline

6. C o n t r a s t between blurred and contoured forms (i.e., line as itself (5), but also as contour, which itself has in addition the effect of pure line).

7. The r u n n i n g - o v e r of colour beyond the boundaries of form.

8. The p r e d o m i n a n c e of colour over form.

9. R e s o l u t i o n s.

March 1911

Wassily Kandinsky

Footnotes

Note: sources referred to in abbreviated form in the footnotes are cited in full in the select bibliography.

1 Cat. Raisonné, No. 367. On the provenance and dating of *Cossacks*, see also Ronald Alley, *Catalogue of the Tate Gallery's Collection of Modern Art*, London, 1981, pp. 379–381.

2 Cat. Raisonné, No. 383. According to Roethel and Benjamin, *Cossacks* was entered in Kandinsky's house catalogues under the date 13 January 1911, while *Composition 4* was dated to the end of February; see Cat. Raisonné, pp. 347, 366.

3 *Writings*, p. 367.

4 Ibid., p. 218.

5 *Composition 5* (1911): Cat. Raisonné, No. 400; *Composition 6* (1913): Cat. Raisonné, No. 464; *Composition 7* (1913): Cat. Raisonné, No. 476. Compare, however, Kandinsky's now destroyed *Composition 2* (Cat. Raisonné, No. 334) with the painting to which he gave the title 'Skizze zu Composition II (Fragment)' (Cat.

Raisonné, No. 325).

6 This aspect of Kandinsky's drawings is discussed in more detail in the article by Vivian Endicott Barnett, 'Kandinsky: From Drawing and Watercolour to Oil', in: *Drawing*, 3, No. 2 (July 1981), pp. 30–34.

7 Hans Konrad Roethel, *Kandinsky. Das Graphische Werk*, Cologne 1970, Appendix V, p. 416, No. 14; repr. p. 482, fig. 60.

8 Ibid., p. 186, No. 93.

9 Letter of 31 January 1904 to Gabriele Münter, published in the catalogue *Kandinsky. Painting on Glass*, Solomon R. Guggenheim Museum, New York, 1966, p. 12; see also *Writings*, p. 346.

10 *Kandinsky 1901–1913*, Berlin [1913].

11 Translated in *Writings*, pp. 383–391.

12 Guns and other warlike forms play an important role in Kandinsky's paintings at this time. Other examples include *Improvisation 11* of 1910 (Cat. Raisonné, No. 338) and *Improvisation 30* of 1913 (Cat. Raisonné, No. 452). Kandinsky

himself gave the latter painting the alternative title 'Cannons', but in a letter to the collector Arthur Jerome Eddy, he emphasized that he had chosen this title for his 'own use', adding: 'The presence of cannons in the picture could probably be explained by the constant war talk that had been going on ... but I did not intend to give a representation of war; to do so would have required different pictorial means.' (*Writings*, pp. 402–3).

13 *Impression 2 (Moskau)*: Cat. Raisonné, No. 373. Kandinsky's essay, preserved in the Gabriele Münter und Johannes Eichner Stiftung in Munich, emphasises the continuing Russianness of his work at this date, despite the fact that the artist had not lived in Russia for more than a decade. Kandinsky recorded that the picture was a product of the impressions he had received during his autumn 1910 visit to Moscow, impressions so powerful that they 'deprived me of my sleep and robbed

me of my strength, so that often, I nearly fainted away . . . never before have I felt so clearly that everything I clothe in pictorial form is, and only ever has been "Moscow".'

14 A choice example of the critical reaction to Kandinsky's work is to be found in the article by Kurt Küchler which appeared in the *Hamburger Fremdenblatt* on 15 February 1913 in connection with an exhibition of paintings at the Galerie Louis Bock in Hamburg. So extreme was Küchler's language that the review provoked a counter campaign organised by Herwarth Walden, under the title 'Für Kandinsky', in which fellow artists, critics and museum directors voiced their support for Kandinsky and their disgust at Küchler's attack. See *Der Sturm*, 150–151 (March 1913); on Kandinsky's relations with Walden and Der Sturm, see *Oeuvres*, 1984, p.78; also *Writings*, p.286.

15 *Scotsman*, 27 April 1912; quoted after *Oeuvres*, 1984, p.80.

16 The critic in question was Georg Jakob Wolf, writing in *Die Kunst für Alle*, November 1910, pp.68–70; see Peg Weiss, *Kandinsky in Munich. The Formative Jugendstil Years*, Princeton, 1979, p.187, n.143.

17 Hans Hildebrandt, 'Drei Briefe von Kandinsky', in: *Werk*, 42, No.10 (October 1955), p.328 (letter of 25 March 1927).

18 *Writings*, p.396.

19 See Rose-Carol Washton Long, 'Kandinsky and Abstraction: the Role of the Hidden Image', in: *Artforum*, 10, No.10 (June 1972), pp.42–49; also the same author's *Kandinsky. The Development of an Abstract Style*, Oxford, 1980, ch.5 (cited hereafter as Long, 1980).

20 Kandinsky's claim to have painted his first abstract picture in 1911 was first made publicly in his essay 'Selbstcharakteristik', which appeared in Paul Westheim's periodical *Das Kunstblatt* in June 1919 (transl. in *Writings*, pp.430–433). He repeated this claim on a number of occasions, particularly during the 1930s. In 1937, in an interview with the New York dealer and collector Karl Nierendorf, he elaborated further, now asserting not merely that he had painted his first abstract picture in 1911, but that he had created his first abstract *watercolour* in 1910. For a discussion of the dating of Kandinsky's earliest abstract work, see Hans K. Roethel and Jean K. Benjamin, 'A New Light on Kandinsky's First Abstract Painting',

in: *Burlington Magazine*, 119, No.986 (November 1977); compare also *Writings*, p.13 and n.9; p.357 and n.6.

21 The anthology, *Russkie Narodnie Kartinki*, edited by Dmitri Rovinsky, was published in three volumes in St Petersburg in 1881. Washton Long has also pointed to the importance of this collection of religious and folk images in connection with Kandinsky's pre-1914 work: see Long, 1980, especially ch.6.

22 *Glasbild Mit Sonne* (1910): Cat. Raisonné, No.370; *Improvisation 21a* (1911): Cat. Raisonné, No.399; *Kleine Freuden* (1913): Cat. Raisonné, No.466; *Improvisation 26* (1912): Cat. Raisonné, No.429.

23 *Bild mit weissem Rand* (1913): Cat. Raisonné, No.465; for a discussion of the imagery of this painting, see Angelica Zander Rudenstine, *The Guggenheim Museum Collection. Paintings 1880–1945*, New York, 1976, p.256f; also Long, 1980, p.126f.

24 *Improvisation 27* (1912): Cat. Raisonné, No.430; *Study for 'Improvisation 25 (Garden of Love)'*: see Vivian Endicott Barnett, *Kandinsky at the Guggenheim*, New York, 1983, p.91.

25 Pseudonym for Erich Gutkind. The book is entitled *Siderische Geburt. Seraphische Wanderung vom Tode der Welt zur Taufe der Tat*, Berlin, 1910.

26 Letter published in *Arnold Schoenberg – Wassily Kandinsky. Letters, Pictures and Documents*, edited by Jelena Hahl-Koch, London, 1984, pp.55–56.

27 Referred to in Long, 1980, pp.181–182, n.30. Having read Volker's book, Marc's reaction was less than enthusiastic: see *Wassily Kandinsky – Franz Marc. Briefwechsel*, edited by Klaus Lankheit, Munich, 1983, pp.181–182.

28 The mystical books now preserved together with Kandinsky's papers in the Gabriele Münter und Johannes Eichner Stiftung, Munich are listed in an appendix to the article by Sixten Ringbom, 'Art in the "Epoch of the Great Spiritual". Occult Elements in the Early Theory of Abstract Painting', in: *Journal of the Warburg and Courtauld Institutes*, 29 (1966), pp.416–417. See also the same author's *The Sounding Cosmos. A Study in the Spiritualism of Kandinsky and the Genesis of Abstract Painting*, Abo, 1970 for an account of Kandinsky's mystical interests and the influence of occult notions on the development of his art.

29 See footnote 17 above.

30 'Der Gelbe Klang', in: *Der Blaue Reiter*, Munich, 1912, pp.115–131; translated in *Writings*, pp.267–283.

31 See the chronological table published in the monograph by Johannes Eichner, *Kandinsky und Gabriele Münter. Von Ursprüngen moderner Kunst*, Munich [1957], p.203f.

32 *Writings*, p.361.

33 Kandinsky's relations with Lunacharsky and his artistic responsibilities in Russia immediately after the revolution are described in *Oeuvres*, 1984, pp.156–157; see also Sheila Fitzpatrick, *The Commissariat of Enlightenment*, Cambridge, 1970. Kandinsky's programme for the Institute of Artistic Culture is translated in *Writings*, pp.455–472.

34 This suggestion was made by Klaus Brisch in his unpublished dissertation, 'Wassily Kandinsky (1866–1944). Untersuchungen zur Entstehung der gegenstandslosen Malerei an seinem Werk von 1900–1921' (Ph.D., Univ. of Bonn), 1955, and has been followed by most subsequent commentators; see further Long, 1980, p.108f.

35 Nina Kandinsky, *Kandinsky und ich*, Munich 1976, p.235.

36 'Über Bühnenkomposition', in: *Der Blaue Reiter*, Munich, 1912, pp.103–113; translated in *Writings*, pp.257–265.

37 *Writings*, p.364.

38 Ibid, p.889, n.24.

39 Richard Wagner, 'Zukunftsmusik', in: *Gesammelte Schriften und Dichtungen*, Leipzig, 1871–83, Vol.3, pp.163–164.

40 Richard Wagner, *Mein Leben*, Munich, 1911, Pt.III.

41 *Writings*, p.364.

42 Ibid, pp.204–205.

43 Cat. Raisonné, No.503; repr. in colour, p.502.

44 The comparison, referred to earlier, which Münter draws between the content of *Composition 4* and that of *Composition 2* (see footnote 26 above) is of interest in this context, since it has been suggested (by Brisch and others) that the latter painting also treats the subject of the Garden of Delights in combination with motifs related to the themes of conflict and apocalypse. For a resumé of the arguments regarding the possible eschatological and other references contained in *Composition 2*, see Angelica Zander Rudenstine, *The Guggenheim Museum Collection. Paintings 1880–1945*, New York, 1976, p.228f.

Biographical Outline

1866
Born 4 December in Moscow.

1886
Student of law and economics at Moscow University.

1889
Expedition to Vologda province sponsored by the Imperial Society for Natural Science, Anthropology and Ethnography.

1896
Abandons academic career at Moscow University and moves to Munich to study painting.

1900
Pupil of the *Jugendstil* painter Franz von Stuck at the Munich Academy.

1901
Founds the exhibiting society *Phalanx* and its associated art school; first exhibition of the *Phalanx*, for which Kandinsky designs the poster.

1902
Meets the painter Gabriele Münter, who becomes his companion until 1914.

1903
Phalanx school closes.

1904
Dissolves *Phalanx* society. Trip to North Africa.

1905
Trip to Italy. Elected to jury of *Salon d'Automne*, Paris.

1906–7
Kandinsky and Münter move to Paris, then to Berlin.

1908
Returns to Munich, which remains his principal base until the outbreak of the First World War.

1909
Founds *Neue Künstler-Vereinigung München* (New Artists' Association of Munich). Kandinsky is elected president, his compatriot Alexei von Jawlensky becomes vice-president. First exhibition of the *NKVM*.

1910–11
Second exhibition of the *NKVM* (September 1910) includes Kandinsky's *Composition 2*. Shows fifty-four works at Vladimir Izdebsky's 'Salon 2' exhibition in Odessa; the catalogue contains Kandinsky's essay 'Content and Form', and his translation of the composer Arnold Schoenberg's essay 'On Parallel Octaves and Fifths'.

1911
Kandinsky, Marc, Münter and Alfred Kubin resign from the *NKVM* after disagreement over the showing of Kandinsky's *Composition 5*; they organize the rival 'First Exhibition of the Editors of the *Blue Rider*'. Publication of Kandinsky's treatise *On the Spiritual in Art*.

1912
Contents of first *Blue Rider* exhibition form part of the second 'Jack of Diamonds' exhibition in Moscow. Second *Blue Rider* exhibition takes place in Munich. Publication of *Blue Rider Almanac*.

1913
Participates in Herwarth Walden's *Erster Deutscher Herbstsalon* (First German 'Salon d'Automne') in Berlin. To coincide with the exhibition, Walden publishes the album *Kandinsky 1901–1913*; it contains the essay 'Reminiscences', as well as Kandinsky's descriptions of *Composition 4*, *Composition 6* and *Picture with White Edge*.

1914

Second edition of *Der Blaue Reiter* appears. At the outbreak of war, Kandinsky is forced to leave Germany. Spends three months at Goldach in Switzerland, together with Münter. Begins preliminary work on his second major treatise, *Point and Line to Plane*. At the end of the year, returns to Moscow via Odessa.

1915

Meets Münter in Stockholm for Christmas; it is their last meeting.

1916

One-man show at the Gummeson Gallery in Stockholm. Meets Nina Andreevskaia, whom he marries in February the following year.

1917

October Revolution gives Bolsheviks power in Russia. A. Lunacharsky appointed Commissar of Enlightenment.

1918

Kandinsky appointed member of the Visual Arts Department of the Commissariat of Enlightenment, which publishes the Russian version of 'Reminiscences'.

1919

Foundation of Soviet Museums of the Culture of Painting, under Kandinsky's direction. Involved in the reorganization of Russian provincial museums.

1920

InKhuK (Institute of Artistic Culture) established in Moscow under Kandinsky's direction; presents pedagogical programme for the Institute to the First Pan-Russian Conference of Teachers and Students.

1922

Appointed vice-president of the Russian Academy of Artistic Sciences. In December, leaves Russia for Berlin.

1923

At the invitation of Gropius, joins staff of the Bauhaus. Participates in the major Bauhaus exhibition held during the summer in Weimar.

1924

Formation of the group known as the 'Blue Four': Kandinsky, Klee, Jawlensky and Feiniger.

1925

Bauhaus moves to Dessau.

1926

Kandinsky's second major treatise, *Point and Line to Plane*, published in the series of 'Bauhaus books'. In December, the periodical *bauhaus* devotes its first issue to Kandinsky to mark his sixtieth birthday.

1928

Mussorgsky's 'Pictures at an Exhibition' performed at the Friedrich-Theater, Dessau, with sets and costumes by Kandinsky.

1930

Participates in the exhibition *Cercle et Carré* in Paris.

1932

Bauhaus moves from Dessau to Berlin.

1933

Bauhaus closed permanently by the Nazis. Kandinsky moves to Paris and takes an apartment and studio in Neuilly.

1937

Interviewed by art dealer Karl Nierendorf, who mounts one-man exhibition of Kandinsky's work in New York. Included in the notorious 'Degenerate Art' exhibition in Munich.

1938

Participates in the exhibition *Abstracte Kunst* held at the Stedelijk Museum in Amsterdam.

1939

Granted French citizenship.

1944

Dies in Neuilly, 13 December.

Select Bibliography

Kandinsky. Catalogue Raisonné of the Oil Paintings. By Hans K. Roethel and Jean K. Benjamin. Volume I (1900–1916), London, 1982. Cited as Cat. Raisonné.

Kandinsky. Complete Writings on Art. Edited by Kenneth C. Lindsay and Peter Vergo. 2 vols., London, 1982. Cited as *Writings.*

Rose-Carol Washton Long, *Kandinsky. The Development of an Abstract Style.* Oxford, 1980. Cited as Long, 1980.

Kandinsky. Oeuvres de Vassily Kandinsky (1866–1944). Catalogue établi par Christian Derouet et Jessica Boissel. Paris, Musée national d'art moderne, Centre Georges Pompidou, 1984. Cited as *Oeuvres,* 1984.

Peg Weiss, *Kandinsky in Munich. The Formative Jugendstil Years.* Princeton, 1979.

Angelica Zander Rudenstine, *The Guggenheim Museum Collection. Paintings 1880–1945,* New York, 1976.

Vivian Endicott Barnett, *Kandinsky at the Guggenheim.* New York, 1983.

Kandinsky. Painting on Glass. Catalogue of an exhibition at the Solomon R. Guggenheim Museum, New York, 1966. With an introduction by Hans Konrad Roethel.

Hans Konrad Roethel, *Kandinsky. Das Graphische Werk.* Cologne, 1970.

Johannes Eichner, *Kandinsky und Gabriele Münter. Von Ursprüngen moderner Kunst.* Munich [1957].

Sixten Ringbom, *The Sounding Cosmos. A Study in the Spiritualism of Kandinsky and the Genesis of Abstract Painting.* Abo, 1970.

Arnold Schoenberg – Wassily Kandinsky. Letters, Pictures and Documents. Edited by Jelena Hahl-Koch. London, 1984.